Feeling

Caring

Sarah Medina

Illustrated by Jo Brooker

www.raintreepublishers.co.uk
Visit our website to find out more information about **Raintree** books.

To order:
☎ Phone 44 (0) 1865 888112
🖹 Send a fax to 44 (0) 1865 314091
💻 Visit the Raintree Bookshop at **www.raintreepublishers.co.uk** to browse our catalogue and order online.

First published in Great Britain by Raintree,
Halley Court, Jordan Hill, Oxford OX2 8EJ,
part of Harcourt Education.
Raintree is a registered trademark of
Harcourt Education Ltd.

© Harcourt Education Ltd 2007
First published in paperback in 2008
The moral right of the proprietor has
been asserted.

Editorial: Dan Nunn, Cassie Mayer and
    Diyan Leake
Design: Joanna Hinton-Malivoire and
    Ron Kamen
Picture research: Erica Newbery
Illustration: Jo Brooker
Production: Duncan Gilbert

Originated by Modern Age
Printed and bound in China by
    South China Printing Company

ISBN 978 1 4062 0638 8 (hardback)
11 10 09 08 07
10 9 8 7 6 5 4 3 2 1

ISBN 978 1 4062 0645 6 (paperback)
12 11 10 09 08
10 9 8 7 6 5 4 3 2 1

British Library Cataloguing in Publication Data
Medina, Sarah
Feelings: Caring
152.4'1

A full catalogue record for this book is available
from the British Library.

Acknowledgements
The publishers would like to thank the following
for permission to reproduce photographs:
Bananastock p. **22A**, **B**, **D**; Getty Images/Taxi
p. **22C**; Getty Images/photodisc p. **6**, **7**,

Every effort has been made to contact copyright
holders of any material reproduced in this book.
Any omissions will be rectified in subsequent
printings if notice is given to the publishers.

**Essex County
Council Libraries**

Contents

Some words are shown in bold, **like this**. They are explained in the glossary on page 23.

What does caring mean?

When you have different feelings, you do or say different things. Caring is like a **feeling**.

angry

proud

sad

When you are caring, you think of how others feel. You do nice things for people.

What happens when I am caring?

When you are caring, you want to be kind to other people.

You think about how you can help them.

Why should I be caring?

When you are caring, you make people feel happy. You make yourself feel good, too!

When you are caring, other people **notice**. This can show them how to be more caring, too.

Is it easy to be caring?

Being caring is great, but it is not always easy! Sometimes you have to remember to be caring.

Think about how nice it feels when someone is caring. Then decide how you can be caring, too.

How can I be caring?

You can be caring in lots of ways. You can help to make breakfast or clean the house.

You can remember to say, "Please" and "Thank you". Try to say something nice to someone every day.

13

Are people always caring?

Sometimes people forget to be caring. They might be too busy.

Be caring to them, anyway. Then they might remember that being caring is best!

Can I help someone to be caring?

If someone is not caring, show them what to do. Think of ways you can be caring together.

If your baby brother is asleep, you
can play quietly so you do not wake
him up.

17

What should I do when someone is caring?

When someone is caring to you, tell them how great it feels. Say a big "Thank you!"

Do something nice for them another time. Then they will know that you care about them, too.

Enjoy being caring!

Being caring is wonderful! It makes other people feel good. It makes you feel great, too.

If someone is caring, be happy. Then pass on the good **feeling**. Be caring to someone else!

What are these feelings?

A

B

C

D

Which of these people look happy?
What are the other people feeling?
Look at page 24 to see the answers.

Picture glossary

feeling
something that you feel
inside. Caring is like
a feeling.

notice
see

Index

Answers to the questions on page 22
The person in picture C looks happy. The other people could be sad, angry, or jealous.

Note to Parents and Teachers
Reading for information is an important part of a child's literacy development. Learning begins with a question about something. Help children think of themselves as investigators and researchers by encouraging their questions about the world around them. Most chapters in this book begin with a question. Read the question together. Look at the pictures. Talk about what you think the answer might be. Then read the text to find out if your predictions were correct. Think of other questions you could ask about the topic, and discuss where you might find the answers. Assist children in using the picture glossary and the index to practice new vocabulary and research skills.